D1565610

LITTLE WONDERS

THE WONDER OF
Little
BOYS

Phyllis Hobe

The C.R. Gibson Company
Norwalk, Connecticut 06856

LITTLE WONDERS

The Wonder of Mom
The Wonder of Dad
The Wonder of Friends
The Wonder of Babies
The Wonder of Little Girls
The Wonder of Little Boys

Published by The C.R. Gibson Company,
Norwalk, Connecticut 06856

Printed in the U.S.A.
Designed by Deborah Michel

ISBN 0-8378-8326-1
GB405

The hardest thing
for little boys to do
is to sit still.

It is absolutely impossible for a little boy to go up or down steps one at a time.

The last thing a little
boy wants to do
is to go shopping...
the next-to-last thing a
little boy wants to do
is to try on new clothes.

Little boys won't tell you
what they like to wear.
Your only clues are
what wears out fast
and what never
gets worn.

Little boys won't tell
you when something is
bothering them,
but they stay close by
when something is
bothering you.

Whatever kinds
of food a little
boy doesn't like,
he will never
try again.

Your little boy
may not want to shovel
your sidewalk, but he'll
shovel a neighbor's
without even
being asked.

Little boys like sleeping
bags better than beds,
they would rather live
in a tent than a house—
but they'll want a ride
in the car to visit the
kid next door.

*L*ittle boys do
not sit in chairs—
they ride them.

After a little boy has to
clean up his room,
he'll stay away from it
as long as possible,
because it isn't
comfortable.

No one has ever
been able to explain
the special bond
between a boy
and a ball.

Little boys can play
games all day, every day,
in any kind of weather,
and will only get
tired after you tell
them to stop.

THE WORST ENEMY OF
LITTLE BOYS IS BOREDOM.

⊷⊶

LITTLE BOYS KEEP
THEIR FRIENDS FOR A
LONG TIME—EVEN THE
ONES THEY FIGHT WITH.

A little boy and grandparents go well together— they make him feel like a big boy, and he makes them feel like kids.

Little boys waiting
for a school bus
look like scrubbed
angels—except to
the bus driver.

There is no challenge as great

as a little boy in school when he

doesn't want to be there...

and no one as courageous

as a teacher who wants to

change his mind.

Little boys can think
of so many things that
are more important to
do than homework.

*L*ittle boys—
think the best thing
about money is the
noise it makes in
their pockets.

There's a hint of big business in the air when little boys are swapping baseball cards.

That noise you hear
in the kitchen on the
morning of your birthday
is your little boy trying to
make your breakfast.

It takes a long
time for a little boy
to get angry, and only
a few seconds to
get over it.

There is no one as lonely as a little boy whose friend has moved away.

Little boys have
to know how things
work, and the only way
to find out is to
take them apart.

Little boys love
horror stories—and
all the gory details.
They feel brave when
you get scared.

LITTLE BOYS SAY,
"SURE," WHEN YOU ASK
THEM TO DO SOMETHING
THEY DON'T WANT TO DO...
THEY ALSO SAY, "SURE,"
EVEN WHEN THEY HAVE NO
INTENTION OF DOING IT.

"Why?" is a little boy's favorite word— as soon as you answer, he'll ask you again.

A little boy feels
little is when he's
sick and big when
you're sick.

Little boys open
their presents slowly
because they're afraid
they won't like what's
inside and won't know
what to say.

It's hard for a little boy to say "I'm sorry"... he's more likely to help you with the dishes without saying anything.

Little boys don't like: writing letters, getting dressed up, tying shoelaces, going to parties, and the little girls who invite them.

Unless you are very agile, every photo you take of your little boy will show him sticking his tongue out or crossing his eyes.

Little boys who don't make the baseball team need a lot of T.L.C.

Don't throw away your little boy's valuable collections— such things as bent nails, keys that don't open anything, a tooth, a rusty belt buckle, and some very ordinary stones.

LITTLE BOYS LIKE:
CARS,
MONSTERS,
CARS,
BUGS,
CARS,
MOTORCYCLES
AND CARS.

You will never
get an answer when
you call a little boy
in to dinner.

Little boys do cry—
they just don't want
anyone to know.

*Y*ou will never
get an answer when
you call a little boy
in to dinner.

Little boys do cry—
they just don't want
anyone to know.

Little boys don't like to talk on the phone—they limit their conversation to "Uh-huh."

There isn't a nicer compliment than a little boy doing something just the way you do.

Little boys don't like to talk on the phone—they limit their conversation to "Uh-huh."

There isn't a nicer compliment than a little boy doing something just the way you do.

You'll be the
last to know that
your little boy has
made honors lists
in school.

A little boy saves all kinds of keys except the one that unlocks the front door.

Even little boys
who do their homework
pretend that they don't.

If you let a
little boy win all the
time, you're creating
a monster.

Little boys like
knots—
they'll tie everything
except their shoelaces.

No one has
yet discovered why
little boys love
baseball caps.

Little boys will blow out all their birthday candles in one breath, even if they turn blue.

Little boys have
more fun emptying
out a sandbox than
playing in it.

The only thing little boys know how to do in the water is splash.

Little boys will laugh at anything except themselves.

Little boys need to know
you're there for them—
but they don't want you
to say it out loud.

Little boys may know the difference between right and wrong, but sometimes they're in such a hurry, they trip over the line.

A little boy's trust
is the highest honor
he can give you.

A little boy has his own way of saying "I love you"—like taking the trash out after you've given up asking...

like combing his hair...
like finishing a meal
before going out to play...
and, once in a while,
not turning away when
you try to kiss him.

It's hard to scold a little boy who's grinning at you.